EXTRAORDINARY CLAIMS
REQUIRE EXTRAORDINARY EVIDENCE.

—CARL SAGAN

EVIDENCE

IDENTIFICATION No. EKJR812

DATE OF COLLECTION: ___ / ___ / ___   TIME OF COLLECTION: _____ ☐ AM ☐ PM

MODE OF COLLECTION:　☐ OBSERVED　☐ OVERHEARD　☐ OTHER _____

LOCATION: _____

TYPE OF EVIDENCE:　☐ PHYSICAL　☐ CIRCUMSTANTIAL　☐ HEARSAY　☐ OTHER

DESCRIPTION: _____

_____

_____

_____

_____

_____

_____

_____

_____

_____

_____

_____

—— ∞ ——

CONCLUSION: _____

_____

_____

_____

_____

_____

. . . AND THE WORLD IS BASICALLY EVIL.

☐ CLEAR AND COMPELLING EVIDENCE　　☐ REASONABLE DOUBT

EXHIBITS

1(a). _____

_____

_____

_____

_____

_____

_____

_____

_____

1(b). _____

_____

_____

_____

_____

_____

_____

_____

_____

_____

_____

_____

EXHIBITS

1(c).

1(d).

EXHIBITS

1(e). _____

_____

_____

_____

_____

_____

_____

_____

_____

1(f). _____

_____

_____

_____

_____

_____

_____

_____

_____

_____

EVIDENCE

DATE OF COLLECTION: /   /   TIME OF COLLECTION: _____ ☐ AM ☐ PM

MODE OF COLLECTION: ☐ OBSERVED   ☐ OVERHEARD   ☐ OTHER _____

LOCATION: _____

TYPE OF EVIDENCE: ☐ PHYSICAL   ☐ CIRCUMSTANTIAL   ☐ HEARSAY   ☐ OTHER

DESCRIPTION: _____

_____

_____

_____

_____

_____

_____

_____

_____

_____

—∞∞∞—

CONCLUSION: _____

_____

_____

_____

_____

_____

_____ . . . AND THE WORLD IS BASICALLY EVIL.

☐ CLEAR AND COMPELLING EVIDENCE   ☐ REASONABLE DOUBT

(AFFIX OR SKETCH EVIDENCE HERE)

ONLY TWO THINGS ARE INFINITE, THE UNIVERSE AND HUMAN STUPIDITY,
AND I'M NOT SURE ABOUT THE FORMER. —ALBERT EINSTEIN

EXHIBITS

2(a).

2(b).

EXHIBITS

2(c). _____

_____

_____

_____

_____

_____

_____

_____

_____

2(d). _____

_____

_____

_____

_____

_____

_____

_____

_____

_____

EXHIBITS

2(e).

2(f).

EVIDENCE

IDENTIFICATION No. EKJR814

DATE OF COLLECTION: /   /   TIME OF COLLECTION: _____ ☐ AM ☐ PM

MODE OF COLLECTION: ☐ OBSERVED   ☐ OVERHEARD   ☐ OTHER _____

LOCATION: _____

TYPE OF EVIDENCE: ☐ PHYSICAL   ☐ CIRCUMSTANTIAL   ☐ HEARSAY   ☐ OTHER

DESCRIPTION: _____

_____

_____

_____

_____

_____

_____

_____

_____

_____

_____

——✸——

CONCLUSION: _____

_____

_____

_____

_____

_____

_____

. . . AND THE WORLD IS BASICALLY EVIL.

☐ CLEAR AND COMPELLING EVIDENCE   ☐ REASONABLE DOUBT

EXHIBITS

3(a).

3(b).

EXHIBITS

3(c).

3(d).

EXHIBITS

3(e).

3(f).

EVIDENCE

IDENTIFICATION No. EKJR815

DATE OF COLLECTION: /   /   TIME OF COLLECTION: _____ □ AM □ PM

MODE OF COLLECTION: □ OBSERVED   □ OVERHEARD   □ OTHER _____

LOCATION: _____

TYPE OF EVIDENCE: □ PHYSICAL □ CIRCUMSTANTIAL □ HEARSAY □ OTHER

DESCRIPTION: _____

CONCLUSION: _____

. . . AND THE WORLD IS BASICALLY EVIL.

□ CLEAR AND COMPELLING EVIDENCE   □ REASONABLE DOUBT

(AFFIX OR SKETCH EVIDENCE HERE)

MAYBE THIS WORLD IS ANOTHER PLANET'S HELL. —ALDOUS HUXLEY

EXHIBITS

4(a).

4(b).

EXHIBITS

4(c).

4(d).

EXHIBITS

4(e).

4(f).

EVIDENCE

IDENTIFICATION No. EKJR816

DATE OF COLLECTION: ___/___/___   TIME OF COLLECTION: _____ ☐ AM ☐ PM

MODE OF COLLECTION: ☐ OBSERVED   ☐ OVERHEARD   ☐ OTHER _____

LOCATION: _____

TYPE OF EVIDENCE: ☐ PHYSICAL   ☐ CIRCUMSTANTIAL   ☐ HEARSAY   ☐ OTHER

DESCRIPTION: _____

_____

_____

_____

_____

_____

_____

_____

_____

———∞∞∞———

CONCLUSION: _____

_____

_____

_____

_____

_____

_____ . . . AND THE WORLD IS BASICALLY EVIL.

☐ CLEAR AND COMPELLING EVIDENCE   ☐ REASONABLE DOUBT

IF I COULD GET MY MEMBERSHIP FEE BACK,
I'D RESIGN FROM THE HUMAN RACE. —FRED ALLEN

EXHIBITS

5(a).

5(b).

EXHIBITS

5(c).

5(d).

EXHIBITS

5(e).

5(f).

EVIDENCE

DATE OF COLLECTION: /   /   TIME OF COLLECTION: _____   □ AM   □ PM

MODE OF COLLECTION: □ OBSERVED   □ OVERHEARD   □ OTHER _____

LOCATION: _____

TYPE OF EVIDENCE: □ PHYSICAL   □ CIRCUMSTANTIAL   □ HEARSAY   □ OTHER

DESCRIPTION: _____

CONCLUSION: _____

_____ . . . AND THE WORLD IS BASICALLY EVIL.

□ CLEAR AND COMPELLING EVIDENCE   □ REASONABLE DOUBT

(AFFIX OR SKETCH EVIDENCE HERE)

EXHIBITS

6(a).

6(b).

EXHIBITS

6(c).

6(d).

EXHIBITS

6(e).

6(f).

EVIDENCE

IDENTIFICATION No. EKJR818

DATE OF COLLECTION: /   /   TIME OF COLLECTION: _____ _____   □ AM
                                                                              □ PM

MODE OF COLLECTION: □ OBSERVED   □ OVERHEARD   □ OTHER _____

LOCATION: _____

TYPE OF EVIDENCE: □ PHYSICAL   □ CIRCUMSTANTIAL   □ HEARSAY   □ OTHER

DESCRIPTION: _____

_____

_____

_____

_____

_____

_____

_____

_____

_____

———∞———

CONCLUSION: _____

_____

_____

_____

_____

_____

_____ . . . AND THE WORLD IS BASICALLY EVIL.

□ CLEAR AND COMPELLING EVIDENCE   □ REASONABLE DOUBT

CYNICISM IS AN UNPLEASANT WAY OF SAYING THE TRUTH. —LILLIAN HELLMAN

EXHIBITS

7(a).

7(b).

EXHIBITS

7(c).

7(d).

EXHIBITS

7(e).

7(f).

EVIDENCE

IDENTIFICATION No. EKJR819

DATE OF COLLECTION: /   /   TIME OF COLLECTION: _____ □ AM / □ PM

MODE OF COLLECTION: □ OBSERVED   □ OVERHEARD   □ OTHER _____

LOCATION: _____

TYPE OF EVIDENCE: □ PHYSICAL   □ CIRCUMSTANTIAL   □ HEARSAY   □ OTHER

DESCRIPTION: _____

_____

_____

_____

_____

_____

_____

_____

_____

—— ∞∞∞ ——

CONCLUSION: _____

_____

_____

_____

_____

_____

_____ . . . AND THE WORLD IS BASICALLY EVIL.

□ CLEAR AND COMPELLING EVIDENCE   □ REASONABLE DOUBT

(AFFIX OR SKETCH EVIDENCE HERE)

EXHIBITS

8(a).

8(b).

EXHIBITS

8(c).

8(d).

EXHIBITS

8(e).

8(f).

EVIDENCE

DATE OF COLLECTION: ___/___/___   TIME OF COLLECTION: _____ □ AM □ PM

MODE OF COLLECTION: □ OBSERVED   □ OVERHEARD   □ OTHER _____

LOCATION: _____

TYPE OF EVIDENCE: □ PHYSICAL □ CIRCUMSTANTIAL □ HEARSAY □ OTHER

DESCRIPTION: _____

_____

_____

_____

_____

_____

_____

_____

_____

_____

—∞∞∞—

CONCLUSION: _____

_____

_____

_____

_____

_____

_____ . . . AND THE WORLD IS BASICALLY EVIL.

□ CLEAR AND COMPELLING EVIDENCE   □ REASONABLE DOUBT

(AFFIX OR SKETCH EVIDENCE HERE)

GOOD AND EVIL ARE VERY HARD TO EXPLAIN OR UNDERSTAND. —KEITH HARING

9(a).

9(b).

EXHIBITS

9(c).

9(d).

9(e).

9(f).

EVIDENCE

IDENTIFICATION No. EKJR821

DATE OF COLLECTION: /   /

TIME OF COLLECTION: _____ ☐ AM ☐ PM

MODE OF COLLECTION: ☐ OBSERVED   ☐ OVERHEARD   ☐ OTHER _____

LOCATION: _____

TYPE OF EVIDENCE: ☐ PHYSICAL   ☐ CIRCUMSTANTIAL   ☐ HEARSAY   ☐ OTHER

DESCRIPTION: _____

_____

_____

_____

_____

_____

_____

_____

_____

—∞∞∞—

CONCLUSION: _____

_____

_____

_____

_____

_____ . . . AND THE WORLD IS BASICALLY EVIL.

☐ CLEAR AND COMPELLING EVIDENCE   ☐ REASONABLE DOUBT

(AFFIX OR SKETCH EVIDENCE HERE)

SUCH IS THE HUMAN RACE. OFTEN IT DOES SEEM SUCH A PITY
THAT NOAH . . . DIDN'T MISS THE BOAT. —MARK TWAIN

EXHIBITS

10(a).

10(b).

EXHIBITS

10(c). _____

_____

_____

_____

_____

_____

_____

_____

_____

_____

10(d). _____

_____

_____

_____

_____

_____

_____

_____

_____

_____

EXHIBITS

10(e).

10(f).

EVIDENCE

DATE OF COLLECTION: ___ / ___ / ___   TIME OF COLLECTION: _____ □ AM □ PM

MODE OF COLLECTION: □ OBSERVED   □ OVERHEARD   □ OTHER _____

LOCATION: _____

TYPE OF EVIDENCE: □ PHYSICAL   □ CIRCUMSTANTIAL   □ HEARSAY   □ OTHER

DESCRIPTION: _____

_____

_____

_____

_____

_____

_____

_____

_____

_____

— ⦵⦵⦵ —

CONCLUSION: _____

_____

_____

_____

_____

_____

_____ . . . AND THE WORLD IS BASICALLY EVIL.

□ CLEAR AND COMPELLING EVIDENCE   □ REASONABLE DOUBT

(AFFIX OR SKETCH EVIDENCE HERE)

EVIL IS UNSPECTACULAR AND ALWAYS HUMAN / AND SHARES OUR
BED AND EATS AT OUR OWN TABLE. —W. H. AUDEN

11(a).

11(b).

EXHIBITS

11(c).

11(d).

11(e).

11(f).

EVIDENCE

DATE OF COLLECTION: /   /

TIME OF COLLECTION: _____ □ AM □ PM

MODE OF COLLECTION: □ OBSERVED   □ OVERHEARD   □ OTHER _____

LOCATION: _____

TYPE OF EVIDENCE: □ PHYSICAL   □ CIRCUMSTANTIAL   □ HEARSAY   □ OTHER

DESCRIPTION: _____

CONCLUSION: _____

... AND THE WORLD IS BASICALLY EVIL.

□ CLEAR AND COMPELLING EVIDENCE   □ REASONABLE DOUBT

(AFFIX OR SKETCH EVIDENCE HERE)

ON THE WHOLE, HUMAN BEINGS WANT TO BE GOOD, BUT NOT TOO GOOD,
AND NOT QUITE ALL THE TIME. —GEORGE ORWELL

EXHIBITS

12(a).

12(b).

EXHIBITS

12(c).

12(d).

12(e).

12(f).

EVIDENCE

IDENTIFICATION No. EKJR824

DATE OF COLLECTION: /   /   TIME OF COLLECTION: _____ ☐ AM ☐ PM

MODE OF COLLECTION: ☐ OBSERVED   ☐ OVERHEARD   ☐ OTHER _____

LOCATION: _____

TYPE OF EVIDENCE: ☐ PHYSICAL   ☐ CIRCUMSTANTIAL   ☐ HEARSAY   ☐ OTHER

DESCRIPTION: _____

⸻⸺⸻

CONCLUSION: _____

. . . AND THE WORLD IS BASICALLY EVIL.

☐ CLEAR AND COMPELLING EVIDENCE   ☐ REASONABLE DOUBT

(AFFIX OR SKETCH EVIDENCE HERE)

EVERY DAY, IN EVERY WAY, THINGS ARE
GETTING WORSE AND WORSE. —WILLIAM F. BUCKLEY

EXHIBITS

13(a).

13(b).

13(c). _____

_____

_____

_____

_____

_____

_____

_____

_____

_____

13(d). _____

_____

_____

_____

_____

_____

_____

_____

_____

_____

EXHIBITS

13(e).

13(f).

EVIDENCE

DATE OF COLLECTION: ___/___/___   TIME OF COLLECTION: _____ ☐ AM ☐ PM

MODE OF COLLECTION: ☐ OBSERVED   ☐ OVERHEARD   ☐ OTHER _____

LOCATION: _____

TYPE OF EVIDENCE: ☐ PHYSICAL   ☐ CIRCUMSTANTIAL   ☐ HEARSAY   ☐ OTHER

DESCRIPTION: _____

_____

_____

_____

_____

_____

_____

_____

_____

_____

—ⴲ—

CONCLUSION: _____

_____

_____

_____

_____

_____

_____ . . . AND THE WORLD IS BASICALLY EVIL.

☐ CLEAR AND COMPELLING EVIDENCE   ☐ REASONABLE DOUBT

(AFFIX OR SKETCH EVIDENCE HERE)

EXHIBITS

14(a).

14(b).

EXHIBITS

14(c).

14(d).

14(e).

14(f).

EVIDENCE

IDENTIFICATION No. EKJR826

DATE OF COLLECTION: /   /   TIME OF COLLECTION: _____ □ AM □ PM

MODE OF COLLECTION: □ OBSERVED   □ OVERHEARD   □ OTHER _____

LOCATION: _____

TYPE OF EVIDENCE: □ PHYSICAL   □ CIRCUMSTANTIAL   □ HEARSAY   □ OTHER

DESCRIPTION: _____

—∞∞∞—

CONCLUSION: _____

. . . AND THE WORLD IS BASICALLY EVIL.

□ CLEAR AND COMPELLING EVIDENCE   □ REASONABLE DOUBT

(AFFIX OR SKETCH EVIDENCE HERE)

EXHIBITS

15(a).

15(b).

EXHIBITS

15(c). _____

_____

_____

_____

_____

_____

_____

_____

15(d). _____

_____

_____

_____

_____

_____

_____

_____

_____

_____

EXHIBITS

15(e).

15(f).

EVIDENCE

DATE OF COLLECTION: ___/___/___   TIME OF COLLECTION: _____ □ AM
□ PM

MODE OF COLLECTION: □ OBSERVED   □ OVERHEARD   □ OTHER _____

LOCATION: _____

TYPE OF EVIDENCE: □ PHYSICAL □ CIRCUMSTANTIAL □ HEARSAY □ OTHER

DESCRIPTION: _____

_____

_____

_____

_____

_____

_____

_____

_____

_____

—∞—

CONCLUSION: _____

_____

_____

_____

_____

_____

_____ . . . AND THE WORLD IS BASICALLY EVIL.

□ CLEAR AND COMPELLING EVIDENCE   □ REASONABLE DOUBT

(AFFIX OR SKETCH EVIDENCE HERE)

EVIL IS OBVIOUS ONLY IN RETROSPECT. —GLORIA STEINEM

EXHIBITS

16(a).

16(b).

EXHIBITS

16(c). _____

16(d). _____

EXHIBITS

16(e).

16(f).

EVIDENCE

DATE OF COLLECTION: ___ / ___ / ___   TIME OF COLLECTION: _____ □ AM □ PM

MODE OF COLLECTION: □ OBSERVED   □ OVERHEARD   □ OTHER _____

LOCATION: _____

TYPE OF EVIDENCE: □ PHYSICAL   □ CIRCUMSTANTIAL   □ HEARSAY   □ OTHER

DESCRIPTION: _____

_____

_____

_____

_____

_____

_____

_____

—⊸∞⊷—

CONCLUSION: _____

_____

_____

_____

_____

_____

_____ . . . AND THE WORLD IS BASICALLY EVIL.

□ CLEAR AND COMPELLING EVIDENCE   □ REASONABLE DOUBT

A CYNIC IS A MAN WHO, WHEN HE SMELLS FLOWERS,
LOOKS AROUND FOR THE COFFIN. —H. L. MENCKEN

EXHIBITS

17(a).

17(b).

EXHIBITS

17(c). _____

_____

_____

_____

_____

_____

_____

_____

_____

_____

17(d). _____

_____

_____

_____

_____

_____

_____

_____

_____

_____

_____

EXHIBITS

17(e).

17(f).

EVIDENCE

IDENTIFICATION No. EKJR829

DATE OF COLLECTION: / /

TIME OF COLLECTION: _____
☐ AM
☐ PM

MODE OF COLLECTION: ☐ OBSERVED ☐ OVERHEARD ☐ OTHER _____

LOCATION: _____

TYPE OF EVIDENCE: ☐ PHYSICAL ☐ CIRCUMSTANTIAL ☐ HEARSAY ☐ OTHER

DESCRIPTION: _____

⸎

CONCLUSION: _____

_____ . . . AND THE WORLD IS BASICALLY EVIL.

☐ CLEAR AND COMPELLING EVIDENCE   ☐ REASONABLE DOUBT

HE WHO LAUGHS HAS NOT YET HEARD THE BAD NEWS. —BERTOLT BRECHT

EXHIBITS

18(a).

18(b).

EXHIBITS

18(c). _____

_____

_____

_____

_____

_____

_____

_____

_____

_____

_____

18(d). _____

_____

_____

_____

_____

_____

_____

_____

_____

_____

_____

_____

EXHIBITS

18(e).

18(f).

EVIDENCE

DATE OF COLLECTION: ___ / ___ / ___

TIME OF COLLECTION: _____ ☐ AM ☐ PM

MODE OF COLLECTION: ☐ OBSERVED ☐ OVERHEARD ☐ OTHER _____

LOCATION: _____

TYPE OF EVIDENCE: ☐ PHYSICAL ☐ CIRCUMSTANTIAL ☐ HEARSAY ☐ OTHER

DESCRIPTION: _____

_____

_____

_____

_____

_____

_____

_____

_____

_____

—∞∞∞—

CONCLUSION: _____

_____

_____

_____

_____

_____

_____ . . . AND THE WORLD IS BASICALLY EVIL.

☐ CLEAR AND COMPELLING EVIDENCE   ☐ REASONABLE DOUBT

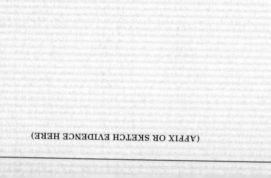

BETWEEN TWO EVILS, I ALWAYS PICK THE ONE I NEVER TRIED BEFORE. —MAE WEST

19(a).

19(b).

EXHIBITS

19(c). _____

19(d). _____

EXHIBITS

19(e).

19(f).

EVIDENCE

IDENTIFICATION No. EKJR831

DATE OF COLLECTION: /   /   TIME OF COLLECTION: _____ ☐ AM ☐ PM

MODE OF COLLECTION: ☐ OBSERVED   ☐ OVERHEARD   ☐ OTHER _____

LOCATION: _____

TYPE OF EVIDENCE: ☐ PHYSICAL   ☐ CIRCUMSTANTIAL   ☐ HEARSAY   ☐ OTHER

DESCRIPTION: _____

—⊂∞∞⊃—

CONCLUSION: _____

_____ . . . AND THE WORLD IS BASICALLY EVIL.

☐ CLEAR AND COMPELLING EVIDENCE   ☐ REASONABLE DOUBT

LIFE IS DIVIDED INTO THE HORRIBLE AND THE MISERABLE. —WOODY ALLEN

EXHIBITS

20(a).

20(b).

EXHIBITS

20(c). _____

_____

_____

_____

_____

_____

_____

_____

_____

_____

20(d). _____

_____

_____

_____

_____

_____

_____

_____

_____

_____

_____

20(e).

20(f).

EVIDENCE

DATE OF COLLECTION: /   /   TIME OF COLLECTION: _____ □ AM
                                                                                    □ PM

MODE OF COLLECTION: □ OBSERVED   □ OVERHEARD   □ OTHER _____

LOCATION: _____

TYPE OF EVIDENCE: □ PHYSICAL □ CIRCUMSTANTIAL □ HEARSAY □ OTHER

DESCRIPTION: _____

_____

_____

_____

_____

_____

_____

_____

_____

_____

⌘

CONCLUSION: _____

_____

_____

_____

_____

_____

_____ . . . AND THE WORLD IS BASICALLY EVIL.

□ CLEAR AND COMPELLING EVIDENCE   □ REASONABLE DOUBT

(AFFIX OR SKETCH EVIDENCE HERE)

THERE IS NOTHING EITHER GOOD OR BAD
BUT THINKING MAKES IT SO. —WILLIAM SHAKESPEARE

EXHIBITS

21(c).

21(d).

EXHIBITS

21(e).

21(f).

Created and published by Knock Knock
1635-B Electric Ave.
Venice, CA 90291
knockknockstuff.com

ISBN: 978-1601067173
UPC: 825703-50206-0